PINSTRIPE
QUOTES

PINSTRIPE QUOTES

The Wit and Wisdom of the
NEW YORK YANKEES

EDITED BY

HENRY CLOUGHERTY

FOREWORD BY **Christopher Jennison**

SPORTS
PUBLISHING

Sports Publishing books may be purchased in bulk at special
discounts for sales promotion, corporate gifts, fund-raising, or
educational purposes. Special editions can also be created to
specifications. For details, contact the Special Sales Department,
Sports Publishing, 307 West 36th Street, 11th Floor, New York,
NY 10018 or sportspubbooks@skyhorsepublishing.com.

Sports Publishing® is a registered trademark of
Skyhorse Publishing, Inc.®, a Delaware corporation.

Visit our website at www.sportspubbooks.com

10 9 8 7 6 5 4 3 2 1

Library of Congress Cataloging-in-Publication Data
is available on file.

ISBN: 978-1-61321-236-3

Printed in China

To my parents, for their patience and understanding while I was striking out.

Contents

Foreword by *Christopher Jennison*   ix

Chapter 1: **The New York Yankees**   1

Chapter 2: **20s and 30s**   27

Chapter 3: **40s and 50s**   47

Chapter 4: **60s, 70s, and 80s**   87

Chapter 5: **90s and 2000s**   111

Chapter 6: **Yankee Wisdom**   143

Foreword

Growing up during the 1950s in a New York suburb, I was a frenzied Yankees fan. I worshiped the team and thought that the players were dignified and invincible. But it never occurred to me that they were funny. From top management to the batboys, serious purpose seemed to be the guiding principle. The players' faces staring out at me from magazines, newspapers, yearbooks, and baseball cards were invariably grim and combative.

Outfielder Hank Bauer, a '50s mainstay, epitomized the culture. His leathery skin and granite jaws sent a "Don't mess with me" message. I don't remember a single picture of him smiling.

Actually, Hank did make a salty comment after the fifth game of the 1955 World Series. The Yankees had lost three straight games to the Brooklyn Dodgers at Ebbets Field, and Hank growled to a reporter, "I'll be glad to get out of this rat trap." But he wasn't trying to be funny.

Even Casey Stengel's erratic double-talk never struck me as amusing. His voice and manner were always cranky. And Yogi Berra, who, in retrospect, has become one of baseball's favorite sources of antic quotes, was the best catcher in baseball during the 1950s, and there was nothing funny about that. His experiments with language and logic were not celebrated until long after his career had ended.

Now, thanks to *Pinstripe Quotes: The Wit and Wisdom of the New York Yankees*, we have, for the first time, a comprehensive source of quotes by and about the Yankees that bring a measure of irreverence to one of professional sport's most magisterial franchises.

Not all of the material selected intends to puncture the team's formidable armor with humor. There are dozens of selections that are reflective and poignant. "I never knew how someone dying could say he was the luckiest man in the world," Mickey Mantle said during his 1969 farewell address, echoing the transcendent words spoken by Lou Gehrig thirty years earlier. Gehrig himself has a brief and prescient remark about racial discrimination quoted in this book. And his unstinting work ethic is revealed in another quote: "The ballplayer who loses his head, who can't keep his cool, is worse than no ballplayer at all."

Today's media battlefield demands quotes and sound-bites hungrily. Derek Jeter's admission that he likes " . . . to dance and sing when there's no one around," made good copy, as did "Gee it's lonesome in the outfield. It's hard to keep awake with nothing to do," a remark made by Babe Ruth. The Babe would have had the last word in any decade. He offered wisdom: "Don't ever forget two things I'm going to tell you. One, don't believe everything that's written about you. Two, don't pick up too many checks." And he defined how we feel about the game when he said, "The only real game in the world, I think, is baseball."

Baseball fans, not just Yankees admirers, will find much to savor in this book. It offers new and unexpected glimpses of a team that continues to intrigue and entertain us no matter what loyalties we espouse.

—Christopher Jennison

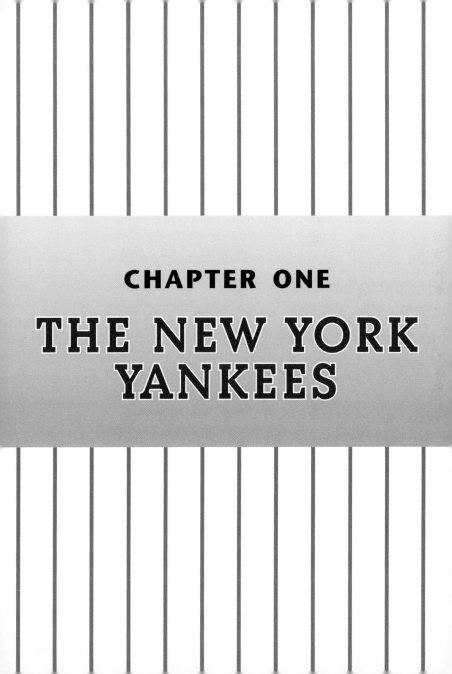

CHAPTER ONE

THE NEW YORK YANKEES

"You have to strap it on and go get them."
—Roger Clemens

"It's great to be young and be a Yankee!"
—Joe DiMaggio

"I want players to look neat and responsible. Maybe it's old school, but it's kind of neat when people are always clean."
—Joe Girardi

"Look, I like hitting fourth and I like the good batting average. But what I do everyday behind the plate is a lot more important because it touches so many more people and so many more aspects of the game."
—Thurman Munson

"You kind of took it for granted around the Yankees that there was always going to be baseball in October."
—Whitey Ford

ACE ROGER CLEMENS, 2007
PHOTO COURTESY OF KEITH ALLISON ON FLICKR

FIRST BASEMAN AND SLUGGER MARK TEIXEIRA
PHOTO COURTESY OF KEITH ALLISON

"Most guys who don't like me are either Democrats or Yankee fans."

—*Curt Schilling*

"I'd like to thank the good Lord for making me a Yankee."

—*Joe DiMaggio*

"All literary men are Red Sox fans—to be a Yankee fan in a literate society is to endanger your life."

—*John Cheever*

"To play 18 years in Yankee Stadium is the best thing that could ever happen to a ballplayer."

—*Mickey Mantle*

"When you go to other parks, they hang banners for the wild-card or Eastern Division or Western Division champions. Around here, they don't hang anything unless its for being world champions."

—*Chili Davis*

"My heroes, my dreams, and my future lay in Yankee Stadium. And they can't take that from me."

—Derek Jeter

"My office is at Yankee Stadium. Yes, dreams do come true."

—Derek Jeter

"To pitch a perfect game wearing pinstripes at Yankee Stadium, it's unbelievable. Growing up a Yankee fan, to come out here and make history, it really is a dream come true."

—David Wells

"Sometimes I think I'm in the greatest business in the world. Then you lose four straight and want to change places with the farmer."

—Joe McCarthy, Yankees Manager

"I may not have been the best Yankee to put on the pinstripes, but I am the proudest."

—Billy Martin

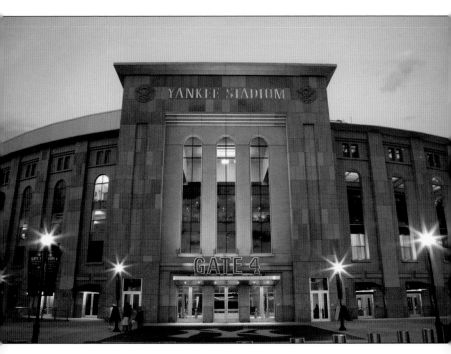

Photo courtesy of eddtoro / Shutterstock.com

SPECIAL WARFARE OPERATOR 1ST CLASS ISAIAH MARING (SEAL)
AND RON GUIDRY, 2010
PHOTO COURTESY OF U.S. NAVY
PHOTO BY SENIOR CHIEF MASS COMMUNICATION SPECIALIST GARY WARD

"You know it as soon as you walk in Yankee Stadium. The electricity is there every time, every day."

—*Nomar Garciaparra*

"Some kids dream of joining the circus, other[s] of becoming a major league baseball player. As a member of the New York Yankees, I've gotten to do both."

—*Graig Nettles*

"The essence of the Yankees is that they win. From in front or from behind, they win. And that's why the history of the New York Yankees is virtually the history of baseball."

—*Dave Anderson,* The New York Times

"Yankee Stadium, and the Yankees are so famous for Mickey Mantle, Joe DiMaggio, Lou Gehrig, all of those guys."

—*Bert Campaneris*

"It's not easy, but I trust my pitches and I trust my teammates behind me."

—*Mariano Rivera*

"I'm a lucky guy and I'm happy to be with the Yankees. And I want to thank everyone for making this night necessary."

—*Yogi Berra (attending a dinner in his honor)*

"The Yankees don't pay me to win every day, just two out of three."

—*Casey Stengel*

"I've played for teams that were family-oriented organizations. They made you feel like family. The Yankees are strictly a business. Baseball is your life and everything else is secondary."

—*Gary Sheffield*

"As I have said many times—my father was a great fan of Bill Dickey's and he certainly loved the Yankees. I hope that he would be pleased."

—*George Steinbrenner*

"Owning the Yankees is like owning the Mona Lisa."

—*George Steinbrenner*

"I would rather beat the Yankees regularly than pitch a no-hit game."

—*Bob Feller*

"I think of the New York City Ballet as the Yankees without George Steinbrenner."

—*John Guare*

"Everybody says we hated the Yankees. We didn't hate the Yankees. We just hated the way they beat us."

—*Al Lopez*

"True Yankees are born, not made."

—*Jay Mohr*

BABE RUTH, 1921
PHOTO COURTESY OF LIBRARY OF CONGRESS

"The myth is that you put a Yankee uniform on a player and he becomes great."
—*Manager Birdie Tebbetts*

"I was happy that I was drafted, and then it was the Yankees and that just made it even better."
—*Nick Johnson*

"My God . . . What are the headlines going to be like on Monday if the Yankees don't make the playoffs?"
—*Wade Boggs*

"The owner of the New York Yankees, Mr. George Steinbrenner, who I had the greatest respect for, I want to thank him for giving me the opportunity to win that special ring in 1996."
—*Wade Boggs*

"Why do the Yankees always win? The other team can't stop looking at the pinstripes."
—*Frank Abagnale*

"Sympathy is something that shouldn't be bestowed upon the Yankees. Apparently it angers them."

—Bob Feller

"Hating the Yankees is as American as pizza pie, unwed mothers, and cheating on your income tax."

—Mike Royko

"Hating the Yankees isn't part of my act. It is one of those exquisite times when life and art are in perfect conjunction."

—White Sox Owner Bill Veeck

"Have faith in the Yankees, my son."
—Ernest Hemingway in The Old Man and the Sea
(1952)

"I imagine rooting for the Yankees is like owning a Yacht."

—Jimmy Cannon

PHOTO COURTESY OF ISTOCKPHOTO/THINKSTOCK

"I'm going to buy the Yankees. I don't know what I'm going to pay for them, but I'm going to buy them."

—Yankee Owner Dan Topping

"In a tough age which called for tough men in baseball, the Yankees were the toughest. They were managed by a perfectionist, bossed by a president who hated second place, and owned by a man who could say, even with a seventeen-game lead in 1936, 'I can't stand the suspense. When are we going to clinch it?'"

—David Voigt in American Baseball *(1970)*

"The more self-centered and egotistical a guy is, the better ballplayer he's going to be. You take a team with twenty-five assholes and I'll show you a pennant. I'll show you the New York Yankees."

—Pitcher Bill 'Spaceman' Lee

"If you're a Yankee fan, or if you're not a Yankee fan—you have to admit, we're winners."

—Paul O'Neill

WORLD SERIES TROPHIES ON DISPLAY IN THE
YANKEE MUSEUM, YANKEE STADIUM, 2009
PHOTO COURTESY OF Y2KCRAZYJOKER4

"One night I was watching a quiz show on TV and the question was, 'Name a baseball team synonymous with winning.' One girl said, 'Dodgers.' The other girl said, 'Giants.' That made me madder than hell. I kept saying, 'Yankees, you dummies.' And of course the answer was the Yankees."

—Billy Martin

"Rooting for the Yankees is like rooting for U.S. Steel."

—Joe E. Lewis

"The secret of success in pitching lies in getting a job with the Yankees."

—Pitcher Waite Hoyt

"Wall Street bankers supposedly back the Yankees; Smith College girls approve of them. God, Brooks Brothers, and United States Steel are believed to be solidly in the Yankees' corner . . . The efficiently triumphant Yankee machine is a great institution, but, as they say, who can fall in love with U.S. Steel?"

—Gay Talese, There Are Fans— And Yankee Fans *(1958)*

"All ballplayers want to wind up their careers with the Cubs, Giants, or Yankees. They just can't help it."

—*Dizzy Dean*

"The reason the Yankees never lay an egg is because they don't operate on chicken feed."

—*Dan Parker*

"Everything you hate about New York as a visitor, you love as a home player."

—*Scott Brosius*

"Out of everybody in the country, how come I was the one playing in Yankee Stadium, standing there with my locker next to Mickey Mantle's, going out to dinner with Bobby Richardson after a game? It was just a great feeling."

—*Tom Tresh, on being part of a championship team as a rookie*

MONUMENT PARK AT YANKEE STADIUM, 2008
PHOTO COURTESY OF LLAHBOCAJ

"There's no way they could bury 12 people out there."

—Bob Kearney, discussing the monuments behind the outfield wall in the old Yankee Stadium

"Never is a concept the Yankees won't ever come across."

—Andy Pettitte

"I won't be active in the day-to-day operations of the ball club at all."

—George Steinbrenner, 1973, upon purchasing the Yankees

"[Jason Giambi] says all the right things, like it's [Derek] Jeter's team. I want to correct him on that—it's my team."

—George Steinbrenner, on first baseman Jason Giambi, a new Yankee at the time

"What can I say—just tip my hat and call the Yankees my daddy."

—Pedro Martinez

"OK, he's a Yankees fan. Now I know why I don't like him."

—*Dave Winer*

"I know a man who is a diamond cutter. He mows the lawn at Yankee Stadium."

—*Henny Youngman*

"The crack of a bat sounded amplified in cavernous Yankee Stadium, sprinkled lightly with fans on a cool September evening."

—*William E. Geist*

"There's a difference between a good player, and a good player in New York."

—*Reggie Jackson*

"The Royals and Yankees hated each other. To this day, whenever I see Lou Piniella or one of those Yankees, we talk about how we hated those guys. One time I didn't even have the ball and [Piniella] tried to spike me at third base."

—*George Brett*

An overview of the "old" Yankee Stadium
Photo courtesy of Silent Wind of Doom at the English language Wikipedia

"Every great team in baseball history will now be compared to these 1998 Yankees. And I predict, that when the game of baseball is finally done, this team will be remembered as the greatest team of all time."

—*Rudolph W. Giuliani*

"And I was wondering why it took so long for me to get to a World Series—4200+ games, 30+ years . . . well, I guess the Good Lord was just waiting for me to put on the pinstripes."

—*Joe Torre*

"After seeing the response to Bernie, I now know Yankees fans are the greatest on earth."

—*Robinson Cano*

"With this club, it doesn't matter where you hit. You're going to have people on base, one through nine."

—*Bernie Williams, 1996*

"It's nice when little teams win. We let you have a few years of that."

—*Adam Sandler, a Yankees fan*

"God, I hope I wear this jersey forever."

—Derek Jeter

"The majority of American males put themselves to sleep by striking out the batting order of the New York Yankees."

—James Thurber

"If I played in New York, they'd name a candy bar after me."

—Reggie Jackson

"Yankee Stadium is my favorite stadium; I'm not going to lie to you. There's a certain feel you get in Yankee Stadium."

—Derek Jeter

"Babe Ruth, what can you say? You are almost speechless when people put your name alongside his name. I wish I can go back in time in meet him. Obviously, he was probably the most important sports figure in the world at that time."
—*Mark McGwire*

"Like those special afternoons in summer when you go to Yankee Stadium at two o'clock in the afternoon for an eight o'clock game. It's so big, so empty, and so silent that you can almost hear the sounds that aren't there."
—*Ray Miller*

"Rooting for the Yankees is like rooting for the house in blackjack."
—*Adam Morrow, quoted in Bill Simmons' "Letters from the Nation," 20 October 2003*

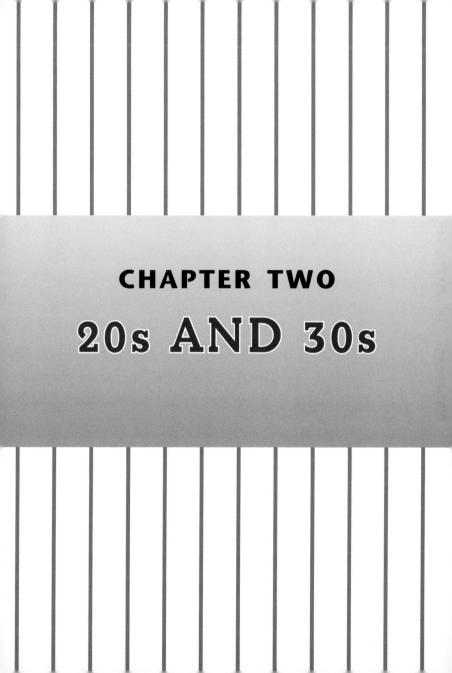

CHAPTER TWO

20s AND 30s

"This isn't just a ballclub. This is Murderer's Row."
—*Arthur Robinson, New York writer*

"[Babe Ruth] had such a beautiful swing, he even looked good striking out."
—*Mark Koenig*

"The greatest name in American sports history is Babe Ruth, a hitter."
—*Ted Williams*

"If it wasn't for baseball, I'd be in either the penitentiary or the cemetery."
—*Babe Ruth*

"I know, but I had a better year than Hoover."
—*Babe Ruth, after being told he was making more money than President Herbert Hoover*

"I don't give a damn about any actors. What good will John Barrymore do you with the bases loaded and two down in a tight ball game? Either I get the money [more than Barrymore], or I don't play!"
—*Babe Ruth*

"[Gehrig] was the guy who hit all those home runs the year [Babe] Ruth broke the record."
—*Franklin P. Adams*

"Just one. Whenever I hit a home run, I make certain I touch all four bases."
—*Babe Ruth, on his superstitions*

"I really didn't room with the Babe. I roomed with his suitcase."
—*Jimmie Reese, on being roommates with Babe Ruth*

"I'll promise to go easier on drinking and to get to bed earlier, but not for you, fifty thousand dollars, or two-hundred and fifty thousand dollars will I give up women. They're too much fun."
—*Babe Ruth*

"The Babe is one fellow, and I'm another and I could never be exactly like him. I don't try, I just go on as I am in my own right."

—*Lou Gehrig*

"I'd rather be lucky than good."

—*Lefty Gomez (also attributed to Red Barrett)*

"If I'd just tried for them dinkie singles I could've batted around six hundred."

—*Babe Ruth*

"It has been aptly said that while [Babe] Ruth was the Home Run King, [Lou] Gehrig was the Crown Prince. Joe DiMaggio must therefore have been heir apparent."

—*Connie Mack*

"At the time, I did think Babe was pointing to the bleachers, but Frank Crosetti told me no, he put up one finger to indicate he had another strike coming. . . . it was quite extraordinary to see him point, then hit the very next pitch out of the ballpark."

—*Charlie Devens, a recollection of Babe Ruth calling his shot in the 1932 World Series*

"Born? Hell, Babe Ruth wasn't born. [He] fell from a tree."

—*Joe Dugan*

"I hit an inside-the-park home run! I beat it out! Can you believe that?"
—*Babe Ruth, as he returned to the dugout in Detroit when he hit his only inside-the-park home run on July 8, 1927, the year he hit 60 home runs*

"It's always the same. Combs walks. Koenig singles. Ruth hits one out of the park. Gehrig doubles. Lazzeri triples. Then Dugan goes in the dirt on his can."

—*Joe Dugan*

"I won't be happy until we have every boy in America between the ages of six and sixteen wearing a glove and swinging a bat."

—*Babe Ruth*

"There was buried in Ruth humanitarianism beyond belief, an intelligence he was never given credit for, a childish desire to be over-virile, living up to credits given his home-run power—and yet a need for intimate affection and respect, and a feverish desire to play baseball, perform, act and live a life he didn't and couldn't take time to understand."

—*Waite Hoyt, on friend and teammate, Babe Ruth*

"[Ruth] wore a glove for one reason: it was a league custom. The glove would last him a minimum of six years because it rarely made contact with the ball."

—*Fresco Thompson*

"Read about your case of amnesia. Must be a new brand."

—*Babe Ruth's telegram to teammate Waite Hoyt after the two had been out drinking. Hoyt ended his night in the hospital. Newspapers reported that he had "a case of amnesia."*

BABE RUTH, 1921
PHOTO COURTESY OF GEORGE GRANTHAM BAIN / LIBRARY OF CONGRESS

"Don't get me wrong, fellows. I don't mind being called a pr*ck or a c*cks*cker or things like that. I expect that. But lay off the personal stuff."
　　—Babe Ruth, to the New York Giants clubhouse during the 1921 World Series after Giants infielder Johnny Rawlings directed a racial slur at him

"I took the two most expensive aspirins in history."
　　—Wally Pipp, on his headache that brought Lou Gehrig into the lineup, prompting the beginning of a new era

"Gehrig had one advantage over me. He was a better ballplayer."
　　—Gil Hodges

"[Gehrig] was there every day at the ballpark bending his back and ready to break his neck to win for his side. He was there day after day and year after year. He never sulked or whined or went into a pot or a huff. He was the answer to a manager's dream."
　　—Sportswriter John Kieran, The New York Times

Lou Gehrig slides into home, 1925
Photo courtesy of The Library of Congress

"Today . . . I consider myself . . . the luckiest man . . . on the face of the Earth."
—Lou Gehrig, in his farewell speech, after he was diagnosed with amyotrophic lateral sclerosis

"Gifted with no flair whatever for the spectacular, except as it might be produced by the solid crash of bat against ball at some tense moment, lost in the honey days of a ballplayer's career in the white glare of the great spotlight that followed Babe Ruth, [Gehrig] nevertheless more than packed his share of the load."
—Bill Corum of the Journal-American

"I did not go there to look at [Gehrig]. I did not even know what position he played, but he played in the outfield against Rutgers and socked a couple of balls a mile. I sat up and took notice . . . I said, here is a kid who can't miss."
—Paul Krichell, long-time Yankees scout

"Handsome, shy, put together along such rugged lines that he was once screen-tested—wrapped in a leopard skin—in Hollywood for the role of Tarzan, a devastating hitter with men on base, Gehrig served perfectly as the idol of a small boy soon to reach adolescence."

—*Frank Graham,* Farewell to Heroes

"I would not have traded two minutes of the joy and the grief with [Lou Gehrig] for two decades of anything with another."

—*Eleanor Gehrig, wife of Lou Gehrig*

"Lou [Gehrig] was the kind of boy that if you had a son, he's the kind of person you'd like your son to be."

—*Sam Jones (the former Yankee)*

"My father looked at the check and then told the scout, 'Throw in another hundred and you can take the rest of the family.'"

—*Joe Dugan, after he signed with the Yankees for 500 dollars*

"When I first signed with the Yankees, the regulars wouldn't talk to you until you were with the team three or four years. Nowadays the rookies get $100,000 to sign and they don't talk to the regulars."

—*Lefty Gomez*

"I don't want to throw him nothing. Maybe he'll just get tired of waiting and leave."

—*Lefty Gomez, when asked what he wanted to throw to slugger Jimmy Foxx*

"When Neil Armstrong first set foot on the moon, he and all the space scientists were puzzled by an unidentifiable white object. I knew immediately what it was. That was a home run ball hit off me in 1937 by Jimmie Foxx."

—*Lefty Gomez*

PHOTO COURTESY OF HEMERA TECHNOLOGIES/PHOTOS.COM/THINKSTOCK

"Lou Gehrig was to baseball what Gary Cooper was to the movies: a figure of unimpeachable integrity, massive and incorruptible, a hero. Today, both are seen as paradigms of manly virtue. Decent and God-fearing, yet strongly charismatic and powerful."

—*Kevin Nelson in* The Greatest Stories Ever Told About Baseball

"The other clubs would do better to stop worrying about breaking up the Yankees and start worrying about catching up to the Yankees."

—*Jacob Ruppert, former Yankees owner*

"Gee, it's lonesome in the outfield. It's hard to keep awake with nothing to do."

—*Babe Ruth*

"Reading isn't good for a ballplayer. Not good for his eyes. If my eyes went bad even a little bit I couldn't hit home runs. So I gave up reading."

—*Babe Ruth,* Babe: The Legend Comes to Life

"I didn't mean to hit the umpire with the dirt, but I did mean to hit that bastard in the stands."

—*Babe Ruth,* The Babe Ruth Story

"Lou Gehrig was a guy who could really hit the ball, was dependable and seemed so durable that many of us thought he could have played forever."

—George Selkirk

"I never heard a crowd boo a homer, but I've heard plenty of boos after a strikeout."

—Babe Ruth

"Paris ain't much of a town."

—Babe Ruth

"Babe Ruth was the greatest baseball player that ever lived. I mean, people say he's less than a God, but more than a man. Like Hercules or something."

—Benny Rodriguez in The Sandlot

"As a rule, people think that if you give boys a football or a baseball or something like that, they naturally become athletes right away. But you can't do that in baseball. You got to start from way down, at the bottom, when the boys are six or seven years of age."

—Babe Ruth

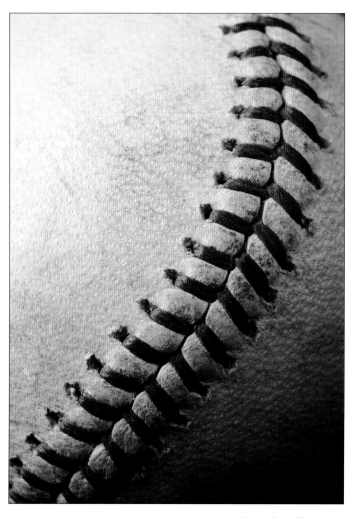

Photo courtesy of iStockphoto/Thinkstock

"The termites have got me."
—*Babe Ruth, referring to his cancer,
the day before he died*

"I hope [Ruth] lives to hit one-hundred homers in a season. I wish him all the luck in the world. He has everybody else, including myself, hopelessly outclassed."
—*Frank Baker*

"A rabbit didn't have to think to know what to do to dodge a dog . . . The same kind of instinct told Babe Ruth what to do and where to be."
—*Sammy Vick*

"I don't recall your name but you sure were a sucker for a high inside curve."
—*Bill Dickey*

"I had a great game against him . . . I held him to three hits."
—*Rollie Stiles, about Babe Ruth*

"Gehrig never learned that a ballplayer couldn't be good every day."

—Hank Gowdy

"No one hit home runs the way Babe [Ruth] did. They were something special. They were like homing pigeons. The ball would leave the bat, pause briefly, suddenly gain its bearings, then take off for the stands."

—Dizzy Dean

"Some twenty years ago I stopped talking about the Babe [Ruth] for the simple reason that I realized that those who had never seen him didn't believe me."

—Tommy Holmes

"Love the game of baseball and baseball will love you."

—Babe Ruth

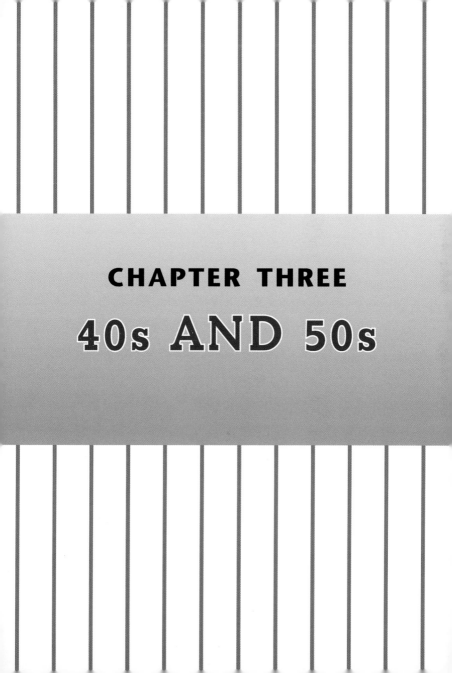

CHAPTER THREE
40s AND 50s

"We need a hit, so here I go."

—Joe DiMaggio

"You can't have a miracle everyday—except when you get great pitching."

—Casey Stengel

"Well, baseball was my whole life. Nothing's ever been as fun as baseball."

—Mickey Mantle

"He's the kind of guy you'd like to kill if he's playing for the other team, but you'd take ten of him on your side."

—Yankees GM Frank Lane, of Billy Martin

"I'm just a ballplayer with one ambition, and that is to give all I've got to help my ball club win. I've never played any other way."

—Joe DiMaggio

"The way to make coaches think you're in shape in the spring is to get a tan."

—*Whitey Ford*

"Mickey Mantle just was everything. At my Bar Mitzvah I had an Oklahoma accent."

—*Billy Crystal*

"You know, Mantle had the greatest ability of any guy who ever came to the big leagues in my time. He didn't have to apply himself. He didn't realize how good he was . . . If he'd have been a little more on determination, like DiMaggio. DiMaggio was a very determined guy, you know."

—*Gene Woodling*

"I'll take any way to get into the Hall of Fame. If they want a batboy, I'll go in as a batboy."

—*Phil Rizzuto*

"The test of an outfielder's skill comes when he has to go against the fence to make a catch."

—*Joe DiMaggio*

"I was such a dangerous hitter I even got intentional walks in batting practice."

—*Casey Stengel, 1967*

"Pardon me, Mr. Craig, but how are we going to defense Mr. McCovey—in the upper deck or the lower deck?"

—*Casey Stengel, to Roger Craig*

"There was an aura about [Joe DiMaggio]. He walked like no one else walked. He did things so easily. He was immaculate in everything he did. Kings of State wanted to meet him and be with him. He carried himself so well. He could fit in any place in the world."

—*Phil Rizzuto*

"I guess heaven needed a shortstop."
—*George Steinbrenner, on the death of Hall of Fame shortstop, long-time broadcaster, and fan favorite, Phil Rizzuto*

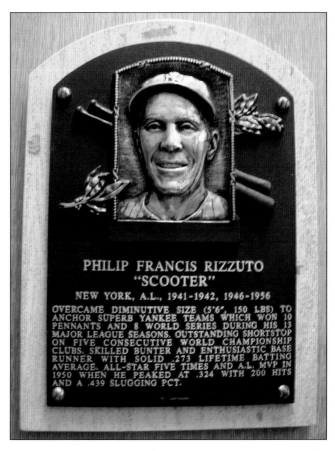

SHORTSTOP PHIL RIZZUTO'S PLAQUE IN COOPERSTOWN. INDUCTED 1994
PHOTO COURTESY OF DELAYWAVES

"Yogisms"

"In baseball, you don't know nothing."

"All pitchers are liars or crybabies."

"A nickel ain't worth a dime anymore."

"I always thought that record would stand until it was broken."

"I don't know [if they were men or women fans running naked across the field]. They had bags over their heads."

"If people don't want to come out to the ballpark, how are you going to stop them?"

"I'm not going to buy my kids an encyclopedia. Let them walk to school like I did."

"It ain't the heat, it's the humility."

"He hits from both sides of the plate. He's amphibious."

"It gets late early out there."

"I can see how he [Sandy Koufax] won twenty-five games. What I don't understand is how he lost five."

"I never said most of the things I said."

CATCHER YOGI BERRA'S PLAQUE IN COOPERSTOWN. INDUCTED 1972
PHOTO COURTESY OF USER R ON EN.WIKIPEDIA

"[Yogi Berra] stopped everything behind the plate and hit everything in front of it."

—*Mel Ott*

"It's like déjà vu all over again."

—*Yogi Berra*

"I like radio better than television because if you make a mistake on radio, they don't know. You can make up anything on the radio."

—*Phil Rizzuto*

"My best pitch is anything the batter grounds, lines or pops in the direction of Phil Rizzuto."

—*Vic Raschi*

"When a fielder gets a pitcher in trouble, the pitcher has to pitch himself out of a slump he isn't in."

—*Casey Stengel*

"You should always go to other people's funerals, otherwise, they won't come to yours."

—*Yogi Berra*

"I wish everybody had the drive [Joe DiMaggio] had. He never did anything wrong on the field. I'd never seen him dive for a ball, everything was a chest-high catch, and he never walked off the field."

—*Yogi Berra*

"Baseball is the champ of them all. Like somebody said, the pay is short and the hours are good."

—*Yogi Berra*

"The towels were so thick there I could hardly close my suitcase."

—*Yogi Berra*

"You can observe a lot just by watching."

—*Yogi Berra*

"We made too many wrong mistakes."

—*Yogi Berra*

"You can't compare me to my father. Our similarities are different."

—Dale Berra

"Yogi, you are from St. Louis, we live in New Jersey, and you played ball in New York. If you go before I do, where would you like me to have you buried?"

—Carmen Berra (Yogi's wife)

"I never blame myself when I'm not hitting. I just blame the bat and if it keeps up, I change bats. After all, if I know it isn't my fault that I'm not hitting, how can I get mad at myself?"

—Yogi Berra

"Yogi had the fastest bat I ever saw. He could hit a ball late, that was already past him, and take it out of the park. The pitchers were afraid of him because he'd hit anything, so they didn't know what to throw. Yogi had them psyched out and he wasn't even trying to psych them out."

—Hector Lopez

"He'd fall in a sewer and come up with a gold watch."

—Casey Stengel, referring to Yogi Berra

"They say he's funny. Well, he has a lovely wife and family, a beautiful home, money in the bank, and he plays golf with millionaires. What's funny about that?"

—Casey Stengel, referring to Yogi Berra

"Why has our pitching been so great? Our catcher, that's why. He looks cumbersome but he's quick as a cat."

—Casey Stengel

"It ain't like football. You can't make up no trick plays."

—Yogi Berra

"If the world were perfect, it wouldn't be."

—Yogi Berra

"You've got to be very careful if you don't know where you're going because you might not get there."

—Yogi Berra

"So I'm ugly. So what? I never saw anyone hit with his face."

—Yogi Berra

"Slump? I ain't in no slump. I just ain't hitting."

—Yogi Berra

"When you come to a fork in the road, take it."

—Yogi Berra to Joe Garagiola, giving directions to his house

"You give 100 percent in the first half of the game, and if that isn't enough in the second half you give what's left."

—Yogi Berra

"Think! How the hell are you gonna think and hit at the same time?"

—*Yogi Berra*

"The wind always seems to blow against catchers when they are running."

—*Yogi Berra*

"You better cut the pizza in four slices because I'm not hungry enough to eat six."

—*Yogi Berra*

"Baseball is 90 percent mental. The other half is physical."

—*Yogi Berra*

"I think Little League is wonderful. It keeps the kids out of the house."

—*Yogi Berra*

"A person always doing his or her best becomes a natural leader, just by example."

—*Joe DiMaggio*

"Whitey [Ford] was a master. It was like watching a pitching textbook in the flesh."

—Yankees pitcher Ralph Terry

"I can remember a reporter asking me for a quote, and I didn't know what a quote was. I thought it was some kind of soft drink."

—Joe DiMaggio

"I would like to take the great DiMaggio fishing, the old man said. They say his father was a fisherman. Maybe he was as poor as we are and would understand."

—Ernest Hemingway, The Old Man and the Sea

"If anyone wants to know why three kids in one family made it to the big leagues, they just had to know how we helped each other and how much we practiced back then. We did it every minute we could."

—Joe DiMaggio

PHOTO COURTESY OF iStockphoto/Thinkstock

"My dad taught me to switch-hit. He and my grandfather, who was left-handed, pitched to me everyday after school in the back yard. I batted lefty against my dad and righty against my granddad."

—*Mickey Mantle*

"I'll never forget September 6, 1950. I got a letter threatening me, Hank Bauer, Yogi Berra, and Johnny Mize. It said if I showed up in uniform against the Red Sox I'd be shot. I turned the letter over to the FBI and told my manager Casey Stengel about it . . . He gave me a different uniform and gave mine to Billy Martin."

—*Phil Rizzuto*

"Do you think I can manage? I have all the credentials, you know. I can really run a game, run a team. I'll do it someday. You'll see."

—*Billy Martin, when he was twenty-one years old, just arriving in New York*

"Now I've had everything except for the thrill of watching Babe Ruth play."

—*Joe DiMaggio*

"Too many kids today are playing major league ball and don't belong there."

—*Joe DiMaggio*

"As far as I'm concerned, [Hank] Aaron is the best ball player of my era. He is to baseball of the last fifteen years what Joe DiMaggio was before him. He's never received the credit he's due."

—*Mickey Mantle*

"I'm glad I don't play anymore. I could never learn all of those handshakes."

—*Phil Rizzuto*

"An outfield composed of [Ty] Cobb, [Tris] Speaker and [Babe] Ruth, even with Ruth, lacks the combined power of [Joe] DiMaggio, [Stan] Musial and [Ted] Williams."

—*Connie Mack*

PHOTO COURTESY OF PHOTODISC/THINKSTOCK

"Baseball didn't really get into my blood until I knocked off that hitting streak. Getting a daily hit became more important to me than eating, drinking or sleeping."
—*Joe DiMaggio, on his record 61-game hitting streak from May 27 to July 25, 1933, in his first full professional season with the San Francisco Seals*

"I don't think anyone can ever put into words the great things [Joe] DiMaggio did. Of all the stars I've known, DiMaggio needed the least coaching."
—*Joe McCarthy*

"As one of nine men, DiMaggio is the best player that ever lived."
—*Connie Mack*

"DiMaggio was the greatest all-around player I ever saw. His career cannot be summed up in numbers and awards. It might sound corny, but he had a profound and lasting impact on the country."
—*Ted Williams*

PHOTO COURTESY OF HERMERA TECHNOLOGIES/THINKSTOCK

"[DiMaggio] had the greatest instinct of any ball player I ever saw, he made the rest of them look like plumbers."

—*Art Passarella*

"[Mickey] Mantle was the only man I ever saw who was crippled who could outdo the world."

—*Casey Stengel*

"There was never a day when I was as good as Joe DiMaggio at his best. Joe was the best, the very best I ever saw."

—*Stan Musial*

"[DiMaggio] was just a smooth outfielder and smooth in his hitting. No mistakes, ever. He was a solid ball player in every way. I never saw him make a mistake, but there was a smooth way he had of going about everything. That's why they put that name on him, The Yankee Clipper."

—*Red Schoendienst*

"In 1960 when Pittsburgh beat us in the World Series, we outscored them 55-27. It was the only time I think the better team lost. I was so disappointed I cried on the plane ride home."
—*Mickey Mantle*

"No man in the history of baseball had as much power as Mickey Mantle. No man. You're not talking about ordinary power. Dave Kingman has power. Willie Mays had power. Then when you're talking about Mickey Mantle—it's an altogether different level. Separates the men from the boys."
—*Manager Billy Martin*

"If I had as many singles as Pete Rose, I'd have worn a dress."
—*Mickey Mantle*

"You saw [DiMaggio] standing out there and you knew you had a pretty darn good chance to win the baseball game."
—*Red Ruffing*

PHOTO COURTESY OF DESIGN PICS/THINKSTOCK

"Hell, if I didn't drink drink or smoke, I'd win twenty games every year. It's easy when you don't drink or smoke or horse around."

—*Whitey Ford*

"The last time around the park. That gave me goose pimples. But I didn't cry. I felt like it. Maybe tonight when I go to bed, I'll think about it. I wish that could happen to every man in America."

—*Mickey Mantle*

"I didn't begin cheating until late in my career, when I needed something to help me survive. I didn't cheat when I won the twenty-five games in 1961. I don't want anybody to get any ideas and take my Cy Young Award away. And I didn't cheat in 1963 when I won twenty-four games. Well, maybe a little."

—*Whitey Ford*

"Sooner or later the arm goes bad. It has to . . . Sooner or later you have to start pitching in pain."

—*Whitey Ford*

"You start chasing a ball and your brain immediately commands your body to 'Run forward, bend, scoop up the ball, peg it to the infield,' then your body says, 'Who me?'"

—*Joe DiMaggio*

"Casey's memory is legendary. It's also inaccurate."

—*Author Ed Linn on Casey Stengel*

"I don't care what the situation was, how high the stakes were—the bases could be loaded and the pennant riding on every pitch, it never bothered Whitey. He pitched his game. Cool. Craft. Nerves of steel."

—*Mickey Mantle, on Whitey Ford*

"All the ballparks and the big crowds have a certain mystique. You feel attached, permanently wedded to the sounds that ring out, to the fans chanting your name, even when there are only four or five thousand in the stands on a Wednesday afternoon."

—*Mickey Mantle*

PHOTO COURTESY OF iStockphoto/Thinkstock

"But god-damn, to think you're a .300 hitter and end up at .237 in your last season, then find yourself looking at a lifetime .298 average—it made me want to cry."

—*Mickey Mantle*

"The phrase 'off with the crack of the bat,' while romantic, is really meaningless, since the outfielder should be in motion long before he hears the sound of the ball meeting the bat."

—*Joe DiMaggio*

"You guys are trying to stop [Stan] Musial in fifteen minutes when the National League ain't stopped him in fifteen years."

—*Yogi Berra, during an All-Star game.*

"I'll play baseball for the Army or fight for it, whatever they want me to do."

—*Mickey Mantle*

"It's unbelievable how much you don't know about the game you've been playing all your life."

—*Mickey Mantle*

MICKEY MANTLE PREPARES TO TAKE A SWING
PHOTO COURTESY OF TONY THE MISFIT

"You would be amazed how many important outs
you can get by working the count down to where
the hitter is sure you're going to throw to his
weakness, and then throw to his power instead."
—Whitey Ford

"When I hit a home run I usually didn't care
where it went. So long as it was a home run was
all that mattered."
—Mickey Mantle

"Somebody once asked me if I ever went up to the
plate trying to hit a home run. I said, 'Sure, every
time.'"
—Mickey Mantle

"You don't realize how easy this game is until you
get up in that broadcasting booth."
—Mickey Mantle

STATUE OF MICKEY MANTLE AT BRICKTOWN STADIUM, OKLAHOMA CITY, OKLAHOMA
PHOTO COURTESY OF BROKENTACO / FLICKR.COM

"There is no sound in baseball akin to the sound of Mantle hitting a home run, the crunchy sound of an axe biting into a tree, yet magnified a hundred times in the vast, cavernous, echo making hollows of a ball field."

—Arnold Hano, Baseball Stars of 1958

"The body of a god. Only [Mickey] Mantle's legs are mortal."

—Infielder Jerry Coleman

"When Joe [DiMaggio] came into the clubhouse it was like a senator or president walking in."

—Billy Martin

"Mantle's greatness was built on power and pain. He exuded the first and endured the second."

—Roy Fitzgerald, The Boston Globe

"That kid can hit balls over buildings."

—Casey Stengel, on Mickey Mantle

"They hung the nickname 'The Commerce Comet' on him, except he was faster than a comet. Fastest thing I ever saw."
—*Pitcher Tom Sturdivant, on Mickey Mantle*

"They ought to create a new league for that guy."
—*Jack Harshman, pitcher, Chicago White Sox, on Mickey Mantle*

"Heroes are people who are all good with no bad in them. That's the way I always saw Joe DiMaggio. He was beyond question one of the greatest players of the century."
—*Mickey Mantle*

"They should have come out of the dugout on tippy-toes, holding hands and singing."
—*Mickey Mantle, in 1963, on the Oakland Athletics' new green and gold uniforms*

"Here's the pitch. Mantle swings. There's a tremendous drive going into deep left field! It's going, going! It's over the bleachers . . . over the sign atop the bleachers . . . into the yards of houses across the street! It's got to be one of the longest runs I've ever seen! How about that!"
—*Mel Allen broadcasting Mickey Mantle's 565-foot home run, April 17, 1953*

"[Mantle] should lead the league in everything. With his combination of speed and power he should win the triple batting crown every year. In fact, he should do anything he wants to do."
—*Casey Stengel*

"I could never be a manager. All I have is natural ability."
—*Mickey Mantle*

"To get a better piece of chicken, you'd have to be a rooster."
—*Mickey Mantle, the slogan he came up with but was never used for his fried chicken franchise in 1968*

PHOTO COURTESY OF ISTOCKPHOTO/THINKSTOCK

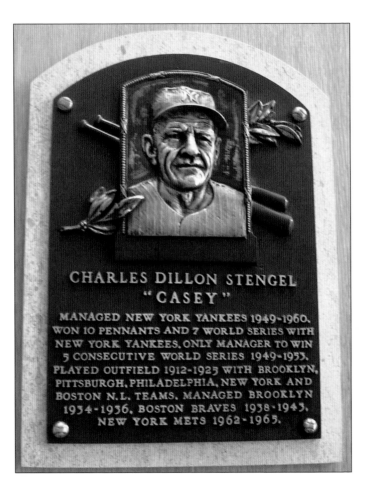

MANAGER CASEY STENGEL PLAQUE IN COOPERSTOWN. INDUCTED 1966
PHOTO COURTESY OF R ON EN.WIKIPEDIA

"Whitey and I figured out once that each year
I hit about 15 long outs at Yankee Stadium that
would have been home runs at Ebbets Field. In
my 18 years I would have gotten 270 home runs
if I'd been a Dodger."

—Mickey Mantle

"Jerry Lumpe looks like the best hitter in the
world until you put him in the lineup."

—Casey Stengel

"Well, God is certainly getting an earful tonight."
—Sportswriter Jim Murray on Casey Stengel's passing

"Why shouldn't he break Ruth's record? He's got
more power than Stalin."

*—Casey Stengel, about Roger Maris after the 1960
season*

"The best team I ever saw, and I really mean this,
was the '61 Yankees. I never got to see the '27
Yankees. Everyone says that was the greatest team
ever, but I think it would've been a great series if
we'd have had the chance to play them."

—Mickey Mantle

"I couldn't have done it without my players."
—*Casey Stengel, on his success with the Yankees*

"I hated to bat against [Don] Drysdale. After he hit you he'd come around, look at the bruise on your arm and say, 'Do you want me to sign it?'"
—*Mickey Mantle*

"Everyone asks how I felt before the perfect game. You never feel bad when you're in the World Series. You've got all winter to rest."
—*Don Larsen, about his perfect game in the 1956 World Series*

"It was all I lived for, to play baseball."
—*Mickey Mantle*

"Joe DiMaggio batting sometimes gave the impression, the suggestion that the old rules and dimensions of baseball no longer applied to him, and that the game had at last grown unfairly easy."
—*Donald Hall*

"DiMaggio seldom showed emotion. One day after striking out, he came into the dugout and kicked the ball bag. We all went 'ooooh.' It really hurt. He sat down and the sweat popped out on his forehead and he clenched his fists without ever saying a word. Everybody wanted to howl, but he was a god. You don't laugh at gods."

—*Jerry Coleman*

"Sometimes I think if I had the same body and the same natural ability and someone else's brain, who knows how good a player I might have been."

—*Mickey Mantle*

"I feel like I have reached the stage where I can no longer produce for my club, my manager, and my teammates…I was full of aches and pains and it had become a chore for me to play. When baseball is no longer fun, it's no longer a game."

—*Joe DiMaggio*

"I'm a vice president in charge of special marketing. That means I play golf and go to cocktail parties. I'm pretty good at my job."

—*Mickey Mantle, on his job with an Atlantic City casino*

"If I knew I was going to live this long, I'd have taken better care of myself."

—*Mickey Mantle*

"I'll never make the mistake of being seventy years old again."

—*Casey Stengel after being fired due to his age*

"There's always some youngster coming up—they'll find somebody . . ."

—*Joe DiMaggio, when asked who would replace him in 1952. That youngster was Mickey Mantle.*

"It was said that the first book Mickey Mantle ever finished was his own autobiography."

—*Joseph McBride, author*

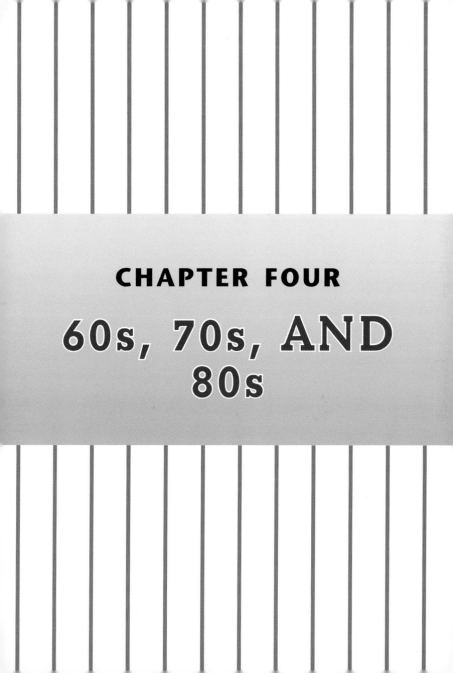

CHAPTER FOUR

60s, 70s, AND 80s

"You measure the value of a ballplayer on how many fannies he puts in the seats."

—George Steinbrenner

"Baseball is a fun game. It beats working for a living."

—Phil Linz

"I don't know if I want to go to New York. They'll have to pay me a lot more money because I like it here in Kansas City."

—Roger Maris

"Hitters always have the fear that one pitch might get away from him [Rich Gossage] and they'll wind up DOA with a tag on their toe."

—Pitcher Rudy May on Goose Gossage

"It's a fickle town [New York], a tough town. They getcha, boy. They don't let you escape with minor scratches and bruises. They put scars on you here."

—Reggie Jackson

"To be a Yankee is a thought in everyone's head and mine. Just walking into Yankee Stadium, chills run through you. I believe there was a higher offer, but no matter how much money is offered, if you want to be a Yankee, you don't think about it."
—*Catfish Hunter, regarding his free agency signing, New Year's Eve 1974*

"I'm glad I don't have to face that guy every day. [Don Mattingly] has that look that few hitters have. I don't know if it's his stance, his eyes or what, but you can tell he means business."
—*Dwight Gooden*

"I like being close to the bats."
—*Don Mattingly, after moving his locker*

"I was reminded [by Jim Bouton] that when we lose and I strike out, a billion people in China don't care."
—*Reggie Jackson*

"A Humble Man of Grace and Dignity. A Captain Who Led by Example. Proud of the Pinstripes Tradition and Dedicated to the Pursuit of Excellence. A Yankee Forever."
 —Don Mattingly's plaque in Monument Park at Yankee Stadium

"You know what the difference is between Reggie Jackson and God? God doesn't think he's Reggie Jackson."
 —Catfish Hunter

"When you unwrap a Reggie bar, it tells you how good it is."
 —Catfish Hunter

"If we're going to run away from Toronto, first we've got to catch them and go by them."
 —Catcher Mike Stanley

DON MATTINGLY HANGS HIS HEAD AFTER A STRIKEOUT
PHOTO COURTESY OF JIMMYACK205

"The only players that are having fun are those having a good year, feasting on pitching or blowing down hitters and garnering all the adulation that goes with it. But, if you're not hitting or not throwing well, or are injured, you better look for fun someplace else."

—*Dave Winfield*

"It's not that Reggie is a bad outfielder. He just has trouble judging the ball and picking it up."

—*Manager Billy Martin*

"There isn't enough mustard in the whole world to cover that hot dog."

—*Darold Knowles, on Reggie Jackson*

"This guy is working all week and he brings his son to this show, has to pay $2 to get in, maybe $5 for a picture and then $6 for an autograph. These guys have to think you're a real ass with your head down all the time signing."

—*Don Mattingly*

"Your [Reggie Jackson] first name's white, your second is Hispanic, and your third belongs to a black. No wonder you don't know who you are."
—*Mickey Rivers, Reggie Jackson's full name is Reginald Martinez Jackson*

"After Jackie Robinson the most important black in baseball history is Reggie Jackson, I really mean that."
—*Reggie Jackson*

"I didn't come to New York to be a star. I brought my star with me."
—*Reggie Jackson*

"In the building I live in on Park Avenue there are ten people who could buy the Yankees, but none of them could hit the ball out of Yankee Stadium."
—*Reggie Jackson*

"It was an insurance run, so I hit it to the Prudential Building."
—*Reggie Jackson*

REGGIE JACKSON SMACKS A HOME RUN AT YANKEE STADIUM, 1979
PHOTO COURTESY OF JIM ACCORDINO

"God do I love to hit that little round son-of-a-bitch out of the park and make 'em say 'Wow!'"

—Reggie Jackson

"Hitting is better than sex."

—Reggie Jackson

"Trying to hit Phil Niekro is like trying to eat Jell-O with chop-sticks. Once in a while you might get a piece, but most of the time you go hungry."

—Bobby Murcer

"I never heard of [Lou] Gehrig before I came here and I always thought Babe Ruth was a cartoon character. I really did. I mean, I wasn't born until 1961 and I grew up in Indiana."

—Don Mattingly

"When they operated, I told them to put in a Koufax fastball. They did—but it was Mrs. Koufax's."

—Tommy John, on his revolutionary arm surgery

"I couldn't quit, because of all the kids, and the blacks, and the little people pulling for me. I represent both the underdog and the overdog in our society."

—*Reggie Jackson*

"I'm human and I've played my butt off for ten years. I'm not a loafer, I'm not a jerk, I'm a baseball player."

—*Reggie Jackson*

"The thing about Reggie [Jackson] is that you know he's going to produce. And if he doesn't, he's going to talk enough to make people think he's going to produce."

—*Catfish Hunter*

"Good hitters don't just go up and swing. They always have a plan. Call it an educated deduction. You visualize. You're like a good negotiator. You know what you have, you know what he has, then you try to work it out."

—*Dave Winfield*

"If I were sitting down with George Steinbrenner and, based on what Dave Winfield got [paid] for his statistics, I'd have to say, 'George, you and I are about to become partners.'"

—*Joe DiMaggio*

"This team, it all flows through me. I've got to keep it going. I'm the straw that stirs the drink."

—*Reggie Jackson*

"Mark Twain said that politicians, old buildings, and prostitutes become respectable with age. Reggie Jackson would like to make it a foursome."

—*Thomas Boswell,*
How Life Imitates the World Series

"Every time we make trouble, ol' George flies out here from another part of the country and gets in our way. Maybe we should make a lot of trouble, so he'll keep flying out here. Sooner or later, his plane's gonna crash."
—*Dock Ellis, on George Steinbrenner,*
spring training, 1978

"These days baseball is different. You come to Spring Training, you get your legs ready, your arms loose, your agents ready, your lawyer lined up."
—*Dave Winfield (1987)*

"I believe if 'Shoeless' Joe Jackson were playing today, he'd have a shoe contract."
—*Don Mattingly*

"It's like obituaries, when you die they finally give
you good reviews."
—*Roger Maris*

"I never had to cheat, I get them with what I got."
—*Dave Winfield*

"Tom Cruise only makes one or two film
appearances a year. A baseball player can be the
hero or the goat one-hundred and sixty-two times
a year."

—*Dave Winfield*

"They say [Dave Winfield] hit the gull on
purpose. They wouldn't say that if they'd seen the
throws he'd been making all year. It's the first time
he's hit the cutoff man all year."
—*Manager Billy Martin, after Dave Winfield's
arrest in Toronto for animal cruelty for hitting a
seagull with a throw*

PHOTO COURTESY OF ISTOCKPHOTO/THINKSTOCK

"If you approach Billy Martin right, he's okay. I avoid him altogether."

—*Pitcher Ron Guidry*

"Candlestick [Park] was built on the water. It should have been built under it."

—*Roger Maris*

"I think the most privacy I had was when the game was going on."

—*Roger Maris*

FORMER SINGLE-SEASON HOME RUN KING, ROGER MARIS'
PLAQUE IN MONUMENT PARK
PHOTO COURTESY OF PENALE52

"I don't want to be Babe Ruth. He was a great ballplayer. I'm not trying to replace him. The record is there and damn right I want to break it, but that isn't replacing Babe Ruth."

—*Roger Maris*

"[Roger Maris] was not in the classic sense—a Mickey Mantle or Harmon Killebrew or Willie Mays—a power hitter. He was a very good line-drive hitter, who was playing in exactly the right ballpark and hitting just ahead of the exact right cleanup hitter."

—*David Halberstam of ESPN*

"There will never be another Babe Ruth. He was the greatest home run hitter who ever lived. They named a candy bar after him."

—*Reggie Jackson*

RICHARD MICHAEL GOSSAGE
"RICH" "GOOSE"
CHICAGO, A.L., 1972-1976, PITTSBURGH, N.L., 1977
NEW YORK, A.L., 1978-1983, 1989, SAN DIEGO, N.L., 1984-1987
CHICAGO, N.L., 1988, SAN FRANCISCO, N.L., 1989
TEXAS, A.L., 1991, OAKLAND, A.L., 1992-1993, SEATTLE, A.L., 1994
A DOMINANT RELIEF PITCHER WITH A TRADEMARK MOUSTACHE,
WHOSE MENACING GLARE AND EXPLODING FASTBALL INTIMIDATED
BATTERS FOR MORE THAN TWO DECADES. POSTED A 124-107 RECORD
WITH 310 SAVES, 1,502 STRIKEOUTS AND A 3.01 ERA IN 1,002 GAMES,
CLOSING OUT VICTORIES CONVINCINGLY, INCREDIBLY DURABLE,
POSTED 52 SAVES OF AT LEAST SEVEN OUTS. A NINE-TIME ALL-STAR
WHO LED THE A.L. IN SAVES THREE TIMES. PITCHED IN THREE WORLD
SERIES, CLINCHING VICTORY FOR NEW YORK IN 1978.

CLOSER RICHARD "GOOSE" GOSSAGE'S PLAQUE
IN COOPERSTOWN. INDUCTED 2008
PHOTO COURTESY OF DELAYWAVES

"Every hitter likes fastballs, just like everybody likes ice cream. But you don't like it when someone's stuffing it into you by the gallon. That's what it feels like when Nolan Ryan's throwing balls by you."

—*Reggie Jackson*

"I had set the standard for my style of relief pitching so high that when I came back to the rest of the pack, everybody said I was done. I was so aggressive on the mound and thought I could throw the ball by anyone. I was so high up there in terms of how I went about my job and being overpowering."

—*Goose Gossage*

"The Goose [Rich Gossage] should do more pitching and less quacking."

—*George Steinbrenner*

CLOSER GOOSE GOSSAGE DELIVERS ONE OF HIS BLISTERING FASTBALLS
PHOTO COURTESY OF USER PHIL5329 ON EN.WIKIPEDIA

"My goals this season are to hit .300, score 100 runs, and stay injury-prone."

—*Mickey Rivers*

"The only difference between me and those other great Yankees is my skin color."

—*Reggie Jackson*

"I remember the first time I caught [Gossage] he'd gotten behind on the hitter and there was a runner on first, so I step out in front of the plate to say something and he yells, 'Get your ass back there and catch.' Finally I go back, Goose throws three straight strikes and we're out of the inning."

—*Barry Foote*

"Deep to left, Yastrzemski will not get it . . . it's a home run! A three-run homer by Bucky Dent!"

—*Bill White*

"This one by Mattingly . . . Oh hang on to the roof! Goodbye, Home Run! Don Mattingly!!!"
—*Gary Thorne*

"Driven to deep right! It is high! It is far! It iiiiiiiiiiiis GONE! A two run game-winning home run by Jimmy Leyritz! And the Yankees have won the game in 15, 7-5! Yankees win! Theeeee Yankees win!"

—*John Sterling*

"He'd [Reggie Jackson] give you the shirt off his back. Of course, he'd call a press conference to announce it."

—*Catfish Hunter*

"His [Dwight Gooden] reputation preceded him before he got here."

—*Don Mattingly*

"He's spent several years in the majors plus several more with the Pirates."

—Don Mattingly, on pitcher Rick Rhoden

"The players get no respect around here. They (the Yankees) give you money, that's it, not respect. We get constantly dogged and players from other teams love to see that. That's why nobody wants to play here."

—Don Mattingly

"I don't think [Roger Maris] wanted his record to be broken. I think he would be happy for Mark [McGwire] and proud for his accomplishments. He would have been proud of Mark as a player, but I think more so as a person."

—Roger Maris, Jr.

CHAPTER FIVE

90s AND 2000s

"I don't want to be gone. I don't want to be somewhere else. I consider myself a Yankee."
—*Jorge Posada*

"We are part of history. We are something special. We were playing for more than the World Series. Now we have some bragging rights."
—*Bernie Williams after winning the 2000 World Series over the Mets*

"It's [baseball] your work, it's your profession, it's your hobby, but it isn't your life. A lot of other things go into that."
—*Joe Torre*

"The name Derek Jeter is made for stardom. He's got an infectious smile, and he's so handsome and well-behaved. He's just a fine young man who does everything right. He's like Jack Armstrong and Frank Merriwell, guys I grew up rooting for. Some guys come along who just measure up."
—*George Steinbrenner*

"I'm pretty excited, this is a big, big one."
  —*George Steinbrenner, on the Alex Rodriguez trade*

"We don't have one big guy. We have a team full of big guys."

—*Tim Raines*

"That club really became the standard of Yankee excellence. There may have been Yankee teams with better players, more Hall of Famers, but I don't think there ever was a team that had all twenty-five guys contribute to the success the way that team did."

—*Joe Torre, on his 1999 Yankees*

"That's why I'm here, I want that World Series ring."

—*Roger Clemens, at his press conference upon joining the Yankees*

"Derek Jeter is off the disabled list and Chuck Knoblauch is not throwing the ball away. All is right with the world."

—Sarah Jessica Parker

"This is the type of thing that as a kid you dream about. Something I've done in my backyard a hundred times. And you never know if you're going to get the opportunity to do it."

—Scott David Brosius, on his game-winning home run in Game 3 of the 1998 World Series

"We just want to win—that's the bottom line. I think a lot of times people may become content with one championship or a little bit of success, but we don't really reflect on what we've done in the past. We focus on the present."

—Derek Jeter, after winning the 2000 AL pennant, heading into a Subway Series versus the Mets

"If the Mets fans who hate Bernie Williams ever met him, they'd love him."

—Sportswriter Barry Stanton

"What I've learned from Cal [Ripken, Jr.] is to respect the game, respect the fans. Nothing fancy out there. Just do your job."

—*Alex Rodriguez*

"Our [pitching] staff comes from all over. We have a pitcher from Cuba, a pitcher from Japan, a pitcher from Panama, and Boomer Wells is from Mars."

—*Tino Martinez*

"Enjoy your sweat because hard work doesn't guarantee success, but without it, you don't have a chance."

—*Alex Rodriguez*

"Derek (Jeter) told me the ghosts would show up eventually!"

—*Aaron Boone*
(after hitting his home run in 2003 ALCS)

PHOTO COURTESY OF ISTOCKPHOTO/THINKSTOCK

"I'm having a hard time finding a date. I don't trust any women I meet. I'm very skeptical."
                    —*Alex Rodriguez*

"To me, he's the greatest modern-day weapon I have seen or played against. [Rivera] has been the heart and soul of the New York Yankees dynasty."
                    —*Alex Rodriguez to the YES Network,*
                    on Mariano Rivera

"I have the greatest job in the world. Only one person can have it. You have shortstops on other teams—I'm not knocking other teams—but there's only one shortstop on the Yankees."
                    —*Derek Jeter*

"[Jeter's] a natural. Young. Handsome. He can play his ass off, playing shortstop for the Yankees. What more do you want? The fact that he's here in the greatest sports town—greatest city in the world—makes it that much better."
                    —*Spike Lee*

"Leadership is a role you have to earn in order to be effective."

—*Alex Rodriguez*

"The only stage I need is the World Series."

—*Alex Rodriguez*

"If you're going to play at all, you're out to win. Baseball, board games, playing *Jeopardy*, I hate to lose."

—*Derek Jeter*

"There is a difference between image and reputation. Image is nice; reputation is developed over an entire career. Reputation is what I'm searching for."

—*Alex Rodriguez*

"You forget about it whether it was 15-2 or 3-2. It's still a loss. It doesn't matter what the score was if we win tomorrow."

—*Derek Jeter*

ALEX RODRIGUEZ WAITS FOR HIS PITCH, 2008
PHOTO COURTESY OF KEITH ALLISON

ALEX RODRIGUEZ HEADS BACK TO THE DUGOUT, 2005
PHOTO COURTESY OF GOOGIE MAN

"The stadium completes the Yanks, we're nothing without it."

—Andy Pettitte

"I'm not a real vocal guy, but sometimes you need to kick someone in the ass."

—Alex Rodriguez

"My dad had been shortstop when he was in college, and you know, when you're a kid, you want to be just like your dad."

—Derek Jeter

"It's something inside his heart that's bigger than anything. He's got the heart of a lion about to grab something."

—Darryl Strawberry, on David Cone

"This kid, right now, the tougher the situation, the more fire he gets in his eyes. You don't teach that."

—Joe Torre, about Derek Jeter

"You gotta have fun. Regardless of how you look at it, we're playing a game. It's a business, it's our job, but I don't think you can do well unless you're having fun."

—*Derek Jeter*

"I loved the game. I played hard, but I knew I wasn't going to be a great player or an immortal Yankee. I think nobody can forget me now after I hit that one."

—*Jim Leyritz, on his homerun in game four of the 1996 World Series*

"Hanging out with [Jeter] sucks because all the women flock to him. Let's see, he's been on the cover of *GQ*, is rich and famous, hits for average and power and is a helluva nice guy."

—*Tim Raines*

"Not relying on any one guy, but getting contributions from every single person on the roster, that's how we win."

—*Derek Jeter*

DEREK JETER SLAPS ONE OF HIS MANY CAREER HITS
PHOTO COURTESY OF GOOGIE MAN

"I'm not impulsive at all—except about buying clothes. That's my biggest weakness."

—Alex Rodriguez

"[Jeter] gets better every year, that's what's remarkable about him. Some guys are good and stay good. Some guys are good and get better. He reminds me of Kareem. Hubie Brown said that Kareem worked at the beginning of every season to improve some facet of his game. It's that way with the best, whatever the profession. That's the way this kid is."

—Ed Bradley of 60 Minutes

"[Jeter's] basically shy. And I know most people don't see him that way. He's so fluid among people. He knows what he is as far as the matinee idol stuff, and he wears it well. He has no pretenses. He's real. He enjoys himself and makes it easy for others to enjoy him."

—Joe Torre

"I had so much confidence in Rivera that I never bothered to worry when Mo allowed a man or two to get on. I knew somehow he would get out of it."

—*Joe Torre*

"Endowed as [Jeter] is with all that talent, all that money and such impeccable manners—that makes him an anachronism. In this era of boorish athletes, obnoxious fans, greedy owners and shattered myths, here's a hero who's actually polite, and that has to have come from good parenting."

—*Sportswriter Gay Talese*

"[Jeter had] been summoned by the baseball gods; to carry the torch, to help save the team and the stadium and maybe even the game of baseball itself."

—*Peter Richmond in* GQ Magazine, *September 1998*

Derek Jeter crosses home plate after blasting a home run
for his 3000th career hit, July 9th 2011
Photo courtesy of Original author: LawrenceFung;
Derivative work: Delaywaves

"I told [Jeter] early on to avoid the pitfalls that plagued me. New York is a place that can swallow you up if you're not able to handle the pressure of success—and of failure. He handles it with class and dignity."

—*Darryl Strawberry*

"What kind of shortstop is Derek Jeter? Well, a very effective one, to be sure. I think he's a sleeker and leaner model of a Cal Ripken. He's out of the Cal Ripken mold in that he's tall and rangy, has a great arm, covers a lot of ground and he's a great offensive player."

—*Ozzie Smith, Hall of Fame shortstop*

"I know there's an enormous heart in there."

—*Joe Torre, about Andy Pettitte*

"When he was in eighth grade and was about to switch from parochial school to a public school, we sent him over to the Y to play basketball against older kids as a way of toughening him up. He went, but he took his mother with him."

—*Charles Jeter (Derek Jeter's Father)*

"[Tommy Pettitte, my father] coached me as kid. He bought all the books and videos and tried to learn as much about pitching as he could. But once I was in high school, he never tried to be my coach."

—*Andy Pettitte*

"Legend has it that at the age of five, Derek told everybody he would someday be the Yankees starting shortstop. They laughed then; they're cheering now. No position player has made such a vital contribution in his first year in the Bronx since Joe DiMaggio."

—*Keith Olbermann of Fox Sports*

"I love [Jeter's] work ethic. He has a great attitude. He has the qualities that separate superstars from everyday people, and a lot of it is attributable to his great family background."

—*Michael Jordan*

"I really want to be known more as a defensive guy, and take my pitchers to the next level. Every time I go out on the field, I take a lot of pride in what I do at the plate, but I take a lot more pride in what I do behind the plate."

—Jorge Posada

"Growing up, I kind of liked the way [Thurman Munson] played. I didn't see much of him, but I remember him being a leader. I remember him really standing up for his teammates, and that really caught my eye."

—Jorge Posada

"Be respectful. Treat people the way you want to be treated. Respect the lowest rank and the highest rank and you'll never get in trouble."

—Alex Rodriguez

"I'm very proud of my area around the plate. I don't want anyone messing with my dirt."

—Jorge Posada

CATCHER JORGE POSADA, SHORTSTOP DEREK JETER, AND CLOSER
MARIANO RIVERA MEET AT THE MOUND, 2007
PHOTO COURTESY OF KEITH ALLISON

FORMER YANKEE CATCHING GREAT, JORGE POSADA, 2011
PHOTO COURTESY OF KEITH ALLISON

"You have to have all types of players to make a clubhouse great. [Posada's] the fiery guy. When you think about it, Joe Torre is the calming influence, Derek Jeter leads by example and Jorge is the fiery guy. When guys need a little kick, Jorge is always there for them."

—*Joe Girardi, Yankees Bench Coach*
Catcher (1996 – 1999)

"He's the best I've ever been around. Not only the ability to pitch and perform under pressure, but the calm he puts over the clubhouse. He's very important for us because he's a special person."

—*Joe Torre, on Mariano Rivera*

"You're not always going to come through. There's been plenty of times that I haven't. But when I'm in that [key] situation, I feel as though I'm going to produce . . ."

—*Derek Jeter*

"You have to understand what [pitchers] do. That's my job. You have to find a way to get them through the game if they're not feeling good. When everything is going good and they're feeling one-hundred percent, it's my job to keep them that way. And you know what? If I see something, I'm going to let them know."

—*Jorge Posada*

"You know how people always tell you that they've been in baseball for 40 years, 50 years, and things happen every game that they never saw [before]? Well, I've never seen that before. I never saw that before in my life."

—*Yankees Bench Coach Tony Pena's reaction to Johnny Damon's double steal in the 2009 World Series*

"[Jeter's] an incredible talent. I'm a lifetime Baltimore Orioles fan, so he's like my worst nightmare."

—*Ed Norton*

"Winning depends on where you put your priorities. It's usually best to put them over the fence."

—*Jason Giambi*

"What I really enjoy most about catching is the relationship with a pitcher. The most important thing is they can relax when I'm back there and know that I did my job, I did some homework on hitters."

—*Jorge Posada*

"I'm not used to seeing the ball go wherever she wants. As a pitcher, I like to be—I don't want to say perfect, but I want to know what the ball is going to do."

—*Mariano Rivera*

"[Jeter's] legit. He's versatile, you can see him on the cover of *GQ*, then the next week he's on the cover of *Sports Illustrated*. He's focused, he works hard. I'm proud of him, I'm glad we're working together."

—*Michael Jordan*

CLOSER MARIANO RIVERA DELIVERS HIS DEVASTATING
CUTTER TO CLOSE OUT ANOTHER YANKEE WIN, 2008
PHOTO COURTESY OF ANC516 AT EN.WIKIPEDIA

"For me it wasn't the statistics. It was just being in the World Series. Imagine a kid from Panama with my poor background walking into Yankee Stadium for a Series game. No thrill could match that."

—*Mariano Rivera*

"Without question we're talking about the best reliever, in my opinion, in the history of baseball. This guy has become branded with the Yankee logo. People are going to remember this man for so long for what he's done."

—*Yankees GM Brian Cashman, on Mariano Rivera*

"Andy [Pettitte] showed 'em down the stretch, and in the post-season, just as Torre and Tommy [Pettitte, Andy's father] expected he would. With a new $25 million, three-year contract, Andy Pettitte pitches on for Torre, for a man Tommy Pettitte called 'more of a father to him than I am, if you know what I mean.'"

—*Sportswriter Harvey Araton in*
The New York Times *(2000)*

"Andy [Pettitte] hides a lot inside. Whereas Roger [Clemens], Roger lets a bit more of his feelings out."

—*Mel Stottlemyre*

"A summer afternoon of baseball ought to be nothing if not relaxing, and no other player can instill calm in his team's fans as reliably as Mariano Rivera, the game's dominant closer and arguably the best relief pitcher of all time."

—*Buster Olney in* New York Magazine

"I call Mo 'the Equalizer.' I mean, I can't tell you how comforting it felt to have him come in when I left the game."

—*Roger Clemens*

"That's what you do in the postseason; you get it to 'Mo' [Rivera]. You start checking off the innings and try to get him into the ballgame."

—*Jason Giambi*

CLOSER MARIANO RIVERA AND CATCHER JORGE POSADA SHAKE
HANDS AFTER ANOTHER JOB WELL DONE, 2009
PHOTO COURTESY OF KEITH ALLISON

"He's the most mentally tough person I've ever played with."

—*Derek Jeter, on Mariano Rivera*

"I see the hitter when he's moved in the box, like when he's moved closer to the plate or changed his stance. I see when the batter has moved his feet, and then I make my own adjustment."

—*Mariano Rivera*

"When [Mariano Rivera] throws it, you think it's straight, and the next thing you know, it's on your thumbs."

—*Tony Womack, St. Louis Infielder, in* New York Magazine

"Reminded me of myself a long time ago."

—*Dwight Gooden, on Mariano Rivera*

"Whatever I do, I love to win. I don't care if it's tennis or ping pong, I'll kill myself to win it."

—*Andy Pettitte*

"When Rivera takes the mound, the other team is sitting in the dugout thinking, 'We've got no chance. It's over.' This guy walks into the game, and they are done."

— *Goose Gossage in* New York Magazine

"[Pettitte's] not afraid to challenge you. What makes him scary is that he's left-handed and the ball comes in on you."

— *Jeff Kent, All-Star Game, 2000*

"Andy is a big game pitcher. That's the bottom line. Every time you think his back is against the wall, he comes out and he does a performance like this. He did it against Texas and he came through again tonight. You can't say enough about him."

— *Derek Jeter, regarding Pettitte's performance in Game 4 of the 1998 World Series*

PLAYOFF BULLDOG ANDY PETTITTE MAKES HIS DELIVERY, 2008
PHOTO COURTESY OF KIDSIRE

"The best deal the Yankees made this year was the one they didn't. That would have been the deal that sent Andy Pettitte to Philadelphia for prospects of dubious promise."
—*Sportswriter Kevin T. Czerwinski in* The Andy Man Can *(1999)*

"What people might find surprising: I taught my wife to change diapers when we had our first."
—*Jorge Posada*

"The Yankees have twenty-five heroes."
—*Derek Jeter*

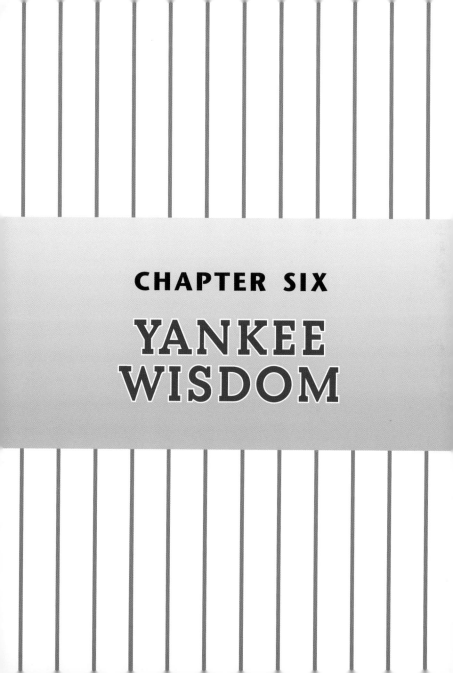

CHAPTER SIX

YANKEE WISDOM

"I'm something like the old soak who never knew whether his wife told him to take one drink and come home at 12, or take 12 and come home at one."

—Lefty Gomez

"Clean living and a fast outfield."

—Lefty Gomez, on the secret to his success

"I love baseball, It's given me everything I have. Look, there are only about six hundred major leaguers in the country. You have to feel special."

—Thurman Munson

"I'm a little too belligerent. I cuss and swear at people. I yell at umpires and maybe I'm a little too tough at home sometimes. I don't sign as many autographs as I should and I haven't always been that good with writers."

—Thurman Munson

THURMAN MUNSON'S LOCKER, PRESERVED IN MEMORIAM IN
THE YANKEES MUSEUM, YANKEE STADIUM
PHOTO COURTESY OF DELAYWAVES

"When you sign on to do a job, you hope you'll be able to get it done. But that's not always in your control."

—*Joe Torre*

"The rules are made by me, but I don't have to follow them."

—*Billy Martin*

"You hit home runs not by chance, but by preparation."

—*Roger Maris*

"I hit big or I miss big. I like to live as big as I can."

—*Babe Ruth*

"Everything looks nicer when you win. The girls are prettier, the cigars taste better. The trees are greener."

—*Billy Martin*

"You play the game to win the game, and not to worry about what's on the back of the baseball card at the end of the year."

—Paul O'Neill

"When you're losing, you see what your team is made of."

—Curtis Granderson

"A baseball club is part of the chemistry of the city. A game isn't just an athletic contest. It's a picnic, a kind of town meeting."

—New York Yankees President Michael Burke

"During the 1920s New York Yankee owner Jacob Ruppert once described his perfect afternoon at Yankee Stadium. 'It's when the Yankees score eight runs in the first inning,' Ruppert said, 'and then slowly pull away.'"

—Peter Golenbock, Dynasty: The New York Yankees *(1975)*

"So many ideas come to you and you want to try them all, but you can't. You're like a mosquito in a nudist colony, you don't know where to start."
            —*Reggie Jackson, on being in a hitting slump*

"As a ballplayer, I would be delighted to do it again. As an individual, I doubt I could possibly go through it again."
            —*Roger Maris, on breaking Babe Ruth's single-season home-run record*

"When you're a professional, you come back, no matter what happened the day before."
            —*Billy Martin*

"Don't find many faults with the umpire. You can't expect him to be as perfect as you are."
            —*Joe McCarthy, Yankees Manager*

"The great thing about baseball is there's a crisis every day."
            —*Yankees General Manager Gabe Paul*

"All right, everyone line up alphabetically
according to your height."
—*Casey Stengel, in spring training*

"Son, we'd like to keep you around this season,
but we're going to try and win a pennant."
—*Casey Stengel to a Yankee rookie*

"Good pitching will always stop good hitting and
vice-versa."
—*Casey Stengel*

"I am dead set against free agency. It can ruin
baseball."
—*George Steinbrenner*

"So I close in saying I may have had a tough
break, but I have an awful lot to live for."
—*Lou Gehrig*

"All I know is, I pass people on the street and they don't know whether to say hello or goodbye."
—Billy Martin during his 3rd term
as Yanks manager

"Pitching is 80 percent of the game, and the other half is hitting and fielding."
—Mickey Rivers

"In the daytime you sat in the dugout and talked about women. At night you went out with women and talked about baseball."
—Waite Hoyt, on baseball in the old days

"The secret of managing a club is to keep the five guys who hate you away from the five guys who are undecided."
—Casey Stengel

"There is always some kid seeing me who may be seeing me for the first or last time. I owe him my best."
—Joe DiMaggio

PHOTO COURTESY OF THINKSTOCK IMAGES

"A ball player's got to be kept hungry to become a big-leaguer. That's why no boy from a rich family ever made the big leagues."

—Joe DiMaggio

"Now there's three things that can happen in a ball game: You can win, you can lose, or it can rain."

—Casey Stengel

"I worked real hard to learn to play first. In the beginning, I used to make one terrible play a game. Then, I got so I'd make one a week, and finally, I'd pull a real bad one maybe once a month. At the end, I was trying to keep it down to one a season."

—Lou Gehrig

"You spend a good piece of your life gripping a baseball, and in the end it turns out that it was the other way around all the time."

—Jim Bouton

"Sometimes the hitter [gets] a hit, sometimes I strike them out, but in neither case does anyone die."

—Orlando "El Duque" Hernandez

"Hitters get paid a lot of money to hit. Let's face it, man, sometimes they just do."

—Andy Pettitte

"Managing is getting paid for home runs that someone else hits."

—Casey Stengel

"I talked to the ball a lot of times in my career. I yelled, 'Go foul. Go foul.'"

—Lefty Gomez

"You always get a special kick on Opening Day, no matter how many you go through. You look forward to it like a birthday party when you're a kid. You think something wonderful is going to happen."

—Joe DiMaggio

PRESIDENT TRUMAN THROWS OUT THE FIRST PITCH ON OPENING DAY, 1951
PHOTO COURTESY OF NATIONAL PARK SERVICE PHOTOGRAPHER ABBIE ROWE

"Everybody judges players different. I judge a player by what he does for his ball club and not by what he does for himself. I think the name of the game is self-sacrifice."

—*Billy Martin*

"I'll never be considered one of the all-time greats, maybe not even one of the all-time goods. But I'm one of the all-time survivors."

—*Jim Kaat*

"Baseball players are smarter than football players. How often do you see a baseball team penalized for too many men on the field?"

—*Jim Bouton*

"If you're not having fun in baseball, you miss the point of everything."

—*Chris Chambliss*

"Sometimes, all of us need to be reminded that this is just a kid's game. We just happen to be grown men playing it."

—*Mike Stanton*

PHOTO COURTESY OF ISTOCKPHOTO/THINKSTOCK

"Lefthanders have more enthusiasm for life. They sleep on the wrong side of the bed and their head gets more stagnant on that side."

—*Casey Stengel*

"Don't be afraid to take risks. Make the most of your journey. Make it fun and exciting."

—*Bernie Williams*

"Never let the fear of striking out keep you from swinging."

—*Babe Ruth*

"Being with a woman all night never hurt no professional baseball player. It's staying up all night looking for a woman that does him in."

—*Casey Stengel*

"I always said I could manage Adolph Hitler, Benito Mussolini, and Hirohito. That doesn't mean I'd like them, but I'd manage them."

—*Billy Martin*

"A lot of things run through your head when you're going in to relieve in a tight spot. One of them was, 'Should I spike myself?'"
—*Lefty Gomez*

"The only clubhouse meetings I like are the ones dividing up playoff shares."
—*Billy Gardner*

"You can't get rich sitting on the bench, but I'm giving it a try."
—*Phil Linz*

"I heard doctors revived a man who had been dead for 4 ½ minutes. When they asked him what it was like being dead, he said it was like listening to Yankees announcer Phil Rizzuto during a rain delay."
—*David Letterman*

"We play today, we win today—that's it."
—*Mariano Duncan*

"You're only as smart as your ERA."

—Jim Bouton

"Fans don't boo nobodies."

—Reggie Jackson

"One thing I've got going for me is I'm a baseball player playing a guitar. I'm not a renowned jazz guitarist. There should be people who are just happy to see me up there playing."

—Bernie Williams

"During my eighteen years I can to bat almost 10,000 times. I struck out about 1,700 times and walked maybe 1,800 times. You figure a ballplayer will average about 500 at bats a season. That means I played seven years in the major leagues without even hitting the ball."

—Mickey Mantle

BERNIE WILLIAMS, 2009
PHOTO COURTESY OF
ORIGINAL VERSION: CHRIS PTACEK
DERIVATIVE WORK: AMINESHAKE

THE BABE RUTH EXHIBIT AT THE YANKEES
MUSEUM, YANKEE STADIUM
PHOTO COURTESY OF Y2KCRAZYJOKER4

"The way a team plays as a whole determines
its success. You may have the greatest bunch of
individual stars in the world, but if they don't play
together, the club won't be worth a dime."

—*Babe Ruth*

"Baseball was, is and always will be to me, the best
game in the world."

—*Babe Ruth,* The Babe Ruth Story

"All I can tell them is pick a good one and sock
it. I get back to the dugout and they ask me what
it was I hit and I tell them I don't know except it
looked good."

—*Babe Ruth*

"As soon as I got out there I felt a strange
relationship with the pitcher's mound. It was as
if I'd been born out there. Pitching just felt like
the most natural thing in the world. Striking out
batters was easy."

—*Babe Ruth*

"There is no room in baseball for discrimination."
—*Lou Gehrig*

"All ballplayers should quit when it starts to feel as if all the baselines run uphill."
—*Babe Ruth*

"Hitting the ball was easy. Running around the bases was the tough part."
—*Mickey Mantle*

"Baseball changes through the years. It gets milder."
—*Babe Ruth,* The Babe Ruth Story

"I don't care who you are, you hear those boos."
—*Mickey Mantle*

"I like to dance and sing when there's no one around, but, if I'm out, I'm really shy about it. So it takes a lot to get me going, but I enjoy being around music."
—*Derek Jeter*

"A team is where a boy can prove his courage on his own. A gang is where a coward goes to hide."
—*Mickey Mantle*

"Don't ever forget two things I'm going to tell you. One, don't believe everything that's written about you. Two, don't pick up too many checks."
—*Babe Ruth*

"The ballplayer who loses his head, who can't keep his cool, is worse than no ballplayer at all."
—*Lou Gehrig*

"If you're going to win games, you're going to have to come up with the big hits. That's the bottom line."
—*Derek Jeter*

"Every strike brings me closer to the next home run."
—*Babe Ruth*

"It's never over. You don't want to be in the position to be down four runs in the ninth inning, but it's not over until the last out."

—*Derek Jeter*

"After I hit a home run I had a habit of running the bases with my head down. I figured the pitcher already felt bad enough without me showing him up rounding the bases."

—*Mickey Mantle*

"I always loved the game, but when my legs weren't hurting it was a lot easier to love."

—*Mickey Mantle*

"You talk about a role model, this is a role model: Don't be like me. God gave me the ability to play baseball and I wasted it."

—*Mickey Mantle*